D1596616

Maxims,

Morals,

and

Metaphors

A Primer on Venture Capital

Scott Chou

This book may be purchased for educational, business, or sales promotional use. For information please write:
Email: schou@alumni.caltech.edu
www.scottchou.com/mmm

First published July 1, 1999
Last updated August 3, 2008

SECOND EDITION

Cover Designed by Bookmasters

Chou, Scott S. (Scott Shouyu), 1964-
　　　Maxims, Morals, and Metaphors: A Primer on Venture Capital / Scott Chou. – 2nd ed.
　　　p. cm.
　　　Includes bibliographical references and index.
　　　ISBN 1-4276-3127-5
　　　1. Business metaphors. 2. Venture capital education. 3. Best practices. 4. Snap judgments. – Management. I. Title

Library of Congress Control Number: 2006925722
ISBN Number: 1-4276-3127-5
ISBN 13 Number: 978-1-4276-3127-5

Published by Aardvark Global Publishing Company, LLC
9587 So. Grandview Dr.　　　　　1-800-614-3578
Salt Lake City, UT 84092 USA

To Stanley

My favorite entrepreneur in training!

– Dad

PREFACE

While experiencing venture capital as an apprenticeship process, I've made a number of observations about the way mentors explain their philosophies and past experiences. One such observation has been the clever use of maxims for achieving profoundness. My first mentor in the venture capital business was Professor Jeffry Timmons, the founding Dean of the Kauffman Fellows Program. For years, Jeff welcomed each incoming class of Kauffman Fellow venture capitalists with his inspirational speech on the *Search for Walter*, which he originally heard at a friend's eulogy. Jeff's passing on April 8, 2008 has been a huge loss to the entire entrepreneurial community. In retrospect on my own experiences, I've come to realize how deep an impression these often humorous expressions can make. As such, I'm dedicating the opening chapter of this book to the memory of Professor Timmons.

This book is a compilation of commonly used aphorisms in the venture capital business and is organized in a manner consistent with the teaching of venture capital as outlined in popular textbooks. Expressions of note are *italicized* and generally offset from the explanatory text. In contrast, consider the encyclopedic approach taken by many business books and the daunting challenge of retention that they impose. I'll be the first to admit that the half-life of most of my academic knowledge has been embarrassingly short. For other readers like me, this book serves to provide longer term retention through wit and wisdom.

Venture capital associates, students of venture capital, and experienced venture capitalists in search of teaching tools are the target audience for this book. If you are an experienced venture capitalist, this book is not so much about learning something new as much as helping you remember what you already know. The objectives of this project will have been met if readers are able internalize some best practices to the subconscious level where they can be relied upon for the innumerable snap business judgments that are typical of the venture capital industry.

Maxims, Morals, and Metaphors was first released on July 1, 1999 as my Kauffman Fellows III field project. Over the years since, I have received hundreds of additional phrases over the Internet from interested readers. I have attempted to capture the best of these submissions in the subsequent releases, but I regret to say that this is a race with a treadmill that I'll never win. Nevertheless, I want to thank the many of you who have written me with ideas and encouragement, and I hope that you'll continue to do so. I also want to thank our fearless founder of Gabriel Venture Partners, Rick Bolander, and his many dedicated troops who helped me proofread the manuscript including Cheryl, Erin, and Tammy. Of course, my wife Tami and son Stanley are the inspiration for my every waking moment. Last but not least, I want to thank the Kauffman Fellows Program for having introduced me to such an exciting industry.

Scott Chou

TABLE OF CONTENTS

Table of Contents

INTRODUCTION

In Search of Walter

So you're thinking about becoming a venture capitalist. Hopefully, you'll learn from this book and help the industry shed any vestiges of its *vulture capital* reputation. This perception paints an unflattering image of greedy financiers who swoop down on cash-starved companies while promising glory, but instead, finish the misery and gobble up the remains. Before you quit your day job, you should consider the scope of your role in the grand scheme of business.

> *Founders are like players.*
> *CEOs are like team captains.*
> *Early stage VCs are like team coaches.*
> *Later stage VCs are like team owners.*

In other words, *do it, run it, teach it, or own it*. It doesn't sound like much but these are important lines to be *drawn in the sand*. One of the easiest mistakes to make is for an entrepreneur-turned-VC to invest in ideas that he/she could do instead of what the management team can do. Nevertheless, most of you who are reading this have probably already

> *crossed over to the darkside*

under the lure of money, influence, and the opportunity to torture entrepreneurs with inane questions. Having done so, you might as well take this opportunity to learn a few tips for the job. Venture capital is very much an apprenticeship trade where you learn on the job. There will be

a lot of roadkill on that road to riches.

It's all about experience and dealing with ambiguity so there won't be a *cookbook* procedure.

You learn from your mistakes but don't become a genius this way.

Good judgment comes from experience, which comes from bad judgment.

If nothing else, your hindsight should be 20/20.

Hindsight will also tell you that the heroes of this business are the ones who do the big deals. The lasting legacy of a great company that you helped create will do more for credibility and deal flow than anything else. *In Search of Walter* refers to the endless attempts by fishermen to catch the mythical great trout that always manages a narrow escape. Likewise, each of you will someday commiserate with other VCs on a fly fishing trip about how you passed on the next Google or eBay.

Don't be content on being average. Being average means you are as near the bottom as you are the top.

DEAL FLOW

Types of Deals

Before starting, it's worth taking a moment to establish some useful deal terminology used in private equity. Some of the more descriptive metaphors for the stages and types of financing include:

Seed	The very first round of seminal financing.
Angels	High net worth individuals who make venture capital investments. Seed round and *angel round* are often used interchangeably.
Startup	The first round of institutional financing. Also known as First or Series A.
Bridge	A transition financing in anticipation of a larger equity financing or acquisition. A word of advice is to make sure you're *financing a bridge and not a pier*. Also, *A Bridge Too Far* is when a struggling company in need of bridge financing will flush *money down the drain* unless substantial equity financing can be found.
Warrant	A right to purchase stock at a future date under specified terms.

Mezzanine	An intermediate financing round that is well after the first but before the exit. It can be either equity or debt.
Subordinated debt	A loan that is lower in liquidation preference to senior creditors. Usually includes warrant coverage to adjust for the additional risk.
Workout	Or a *turnaround*. A financing to restructure an ailing business.
Recap	A recapitalization of the balance sheet. Usually to replace burdensome debt with equity or eliminate prior rounds of equity.
Cramdown	A financing at a significantly lower valuation than prior rounds that will be highly dilutive to prior shareholders. Also known as *down and dirty*.
Pay to play	A follow-on financing in which existing shareholders have their current holdings severely reduced unless they invest a minimum amount such as prorata.
Rollup	An acquisition strategy to merge many smaller businesses into an organization with enough critical mass to achieve operating efficiencies and a significant improvement in valuation.
Buyout	Leveraged buyouts (LBO) and management buyouts (MBO). Financing a change in ownership.
IPO	Initial Public Offering. Practically speaking, it's just another fundraising

event except for the new investors being the general public. You can sell your privately acquired shares only after the *lockup* expires.

PIPE   A private investment in a public entity.

Investment Strategy

Whether you're looking for a firm or getting familiar with one, understanding the firm's investment strategy is a pre-requisite to any deal making. The more straightforward aspects of the strategy include the industry focus, stage, valuation, type of deal, and transaction size.

You are what you eat.

Nothing else establishes your firm's reputation within the venture community more than its deals. Other people will make assumptions on your tastes and expertise based on the types of companies in your portfolio. The nature of your firm's deals will not only determine the type of investment professionals that it attracts but also the investment syndications to which it is invited.

Although a firm's portfolio establishes its public reputation, venture community insiders will form an additional opinion based on how your firm conducts itself during deals. For example, a *trigger-happy* fund can establish a competitive, differentiating factor by deciding very quickly. However, it can be a dubious distinction when poorly managed. Other dubious distinctions include whether you

cut and run at the first sign of trouble
or
rake the entrepreneurs over the coals.

In other words, do you lack the patience to build an industry leader or are you known for having a rough due diligence process? On the other hand, you can *get your hands dirty,* earn the respect of your entrepreneurs, and have the mixed blessing of being known for

> *heel marks at the edge of the cliff*

or funding

> *from womb to tomb*

by supporting companies to the very end. Other factors include whether your firm likes being the *lead dog* on deals or if it prefers to *coattail*. Management style issues include whether your firm is *hands-on* and wants a *seat at the table* or if it just wants *a ticket to the play* where it can observe the outcome without doing the work.

Your firm's investment philosophy may involve issues of a more private nature such as risk averseness.

> *If you're going to swing for the fence, you better be prepared to strike out.*

This is a fundamental aspect of doing high-risk, high-reward deals. However, corollaries include:

> *Strikeouts are no justification for swinging for the fence.*

> *Live by the 3, die by the 3 (pointer).*

You still need to be like Barry Bonds to *knock one out of the park* or Larry Bird to drain from the perimeter. The *shotgun* strategy won't automatically work just because of portfolio theory. It still takes a smart investor to *take open shots* or *pick good pitches* and to have the skills to *carry a deal around the bases*. Portfolio theory also raises significant philosophical issues.

> *Don't put all your eggs in one basket.*

Maxims, Morals, and Metaphors

*Buy enough lottery tickets and you'll
eventually find the right one.*

Sprinkle and sprout

is a very common investment strategy that is fundamentally based on portfolio theory. The idea is that you aren't certain who the winners will be so you spread your money across many investments in small amounts and then pile into the later rounds of the companies that are *getting traction*. When misused by the unskilled venture capitalist, this strategy is also known as

spray and pray.

In either case, both strategies either depend on or suffer from the fact that

lemons ripen faster than plums.

This is not only advice on doing due diligence but it's an essential ingredient in the *sprinkle and sprout* strategy. A small investment in an early round can be viewed as a call option on the company. The theory is that time will buy more information on the company and that time might also weed out the losers. The call option for investors comes in the form of having pro-rata investment rights on future rounds of financing. Another common mistake made when pursuing this strategy is mismanaging the balance of time and money by doing too many small deals.

In for a dime, in for a dollar.

In any case, portfolio theory requires that the good investments pay off really big to cover the losses in the others. This strategy is the most effective in a strong market so it remains a challenge at all other times to minimize your risk by keeping the ratio of losers to winners low. Moreover, a strong IPO market can inadvertently validate what would otherwise be considered questionable investment practices.

*You can't tell who's swimming naked until
after the tide goes out.*

*Don't confuse catching a wave with
causing one.*

In a hot market, it's common for a lot of new money to enter the market by

strapping on venture kneepads.

In this strategy, the fund affiliates itself with strong early stage funds known for turning out successful IPOs. This is usually done by becoming a limited partner in the *feeder funds* or by offering a strategic relationship. A lot of investors will look like geniuses but only those adhering to the fundamentals will survive a market downturn.

Many a slip between the cup and the lip

refers to the perils that can still happen on the eve of a liquidity event. The bursting of the Internet bubble in the spring of 2000 should serve as a reminder to everyone that

all good things do come to an end.

The opposite of *sprinkle and sprout* would be an investment strategy focused on *batting average*. This type of strategy calls for fewer investments and a high survival rate. A fund that plays for batting average is usually characterized by rigorous due diligence and a hands-on approach to management. Although this approach can absorb larger sums of capital while yielding a steady stream of liquidity events for limited partners, it doesn't easily lend itself to investing in homeruns.

Deal Sourcing

The search for Walter starts with getting deals. To make it easy on you in the beginning, you can get deals passively through your firm's existing reputation and marketing efforts. You can always count on the occasional *bluebird* to fly through the door and land on your desk. Nevertheless, there are many ways you can still contribute to these passive marketing efforts such as maximizing your firm's utilization of the web or hiring a PR firm. You may quickly come to the wrong conclusion that generating deal flow is pretty easy.

> *Good ideas are a dime a dozen, bad ones*
> *are free.*

There is a not only a great imbalance between bad ideas and good ideas but also an imbalance between good ideas and the ability to execute them. You'll soon realize that the better deals come through the referral network and that the path to partnership means having your own.

> *Don't wait for your ship to come in, swim*
> *out to it.*

Networking means getting out and meeting with *angels*, other VCs, attorneys, accountants, recruiters, corporate labs, incubators, university licensing offices, etc. You shouldn't limit your search to the obvious places either.

> *Go out and rattle the bushes.*

Speaking engagements at any professional organization can coax a surprising number of entrepreneurs *out of the woodwork*. As for speaking, it is an incredibly important skill to develop for both addressing groups as well as entrepreneurs.

> *Whenever you speak, your brain is on*
> *parade.*

So be aware that whether you're pitching your value-add to a *hot deal* or performing due diligence, the entrepreneur is also interviewing you. If you find networking to be a challenge, rest assured that the private placement community will almost always leave its doors open to you.

> *They call them business brokers because*
> *after a business uses one, it is.*

Well, going broke is an exaggeration but be aware that brokers can charge substantial fees including cash and equity. These fees will reduce the amount of your investment that actually goes to work for the company. The only thing that's for sure when you see a broker is that *the deal has been shopped.* But then it has also been screened and refined to some extent which is similar to the tradeoff you face when reviewing deals at any venture conference.

If you're tired of *chasing the bandwagon* and *paying through the nose* or *eating leftovers*, there is relief. Wayne Gretzky attributed the secret of his success to one simple rule:

> *"I skate to where the puck is going to be,*
> *not to where it has been."*

As a venture capitalist, you'll be exposed to a flood of new ideas that are often a barometer to where markets are moving. It's well within your ability to formulate an investment strategy to identify inexpensive investment opportunities where even the entrepreneurs themselves may not be fully aware of their own potential. For example, firms with incubation strategies have churned out many homeruns based on homegrown ideas. Of course, investing that early calls for *heavy lifting* and the question of

> *incubation or live birth?*

Which is an expression you may want to expand to include *"or childhood or adulthood"* by the time you're through and wished you had the luxuries of being a later stage investor.

Moreover, studies have shown that most successful businesses are not using their original business plan, so there are clearly opportunities for you to create value by finding and developing talent that has been underutilized. Don't get frustrated because it wasn't meant to be easy. You'll have to

kiss a lot of frogs

in your search for Walter.

Screening

After acquiring some business plans, your next step will be to filter out the ones you like. The first and only filter of a cookbook nature will be to match your firm's investment focus. Basic criteria such as geography, industry, capital intensity, consumer orientation, type of financing, and stage should allow you to quickly set aside most of the pile.

We're on a California diet

means the firm prefers to stay close to their offices and invest only on the west coast.

Nothing but net

is a basketball metaphor being used as an industry specialization where the firm focuses only on Internet investments.

I can't raise the water level by pissing in the ocean

is a reference to the capital requirements of a company being too large for the size of the VC fund reviewing it. On the flipside,

you don't need gallons of kerosene to start an inferno.

Which is a great strategy for smaller funds seeking capital efficient businesses that address large, pent up demands.

We're not in the hits business

means that this VC firm isn't like a record or movie producer who assesses whether a product will be a hit amongst consumers. Many VC firms have historically shied away from consumer oriented businesses until the rise of the Internet made the sector too lucrative to avoid.

Leave that one for the bankers

usually means that a company is too late stage for venture capital. In these situations, the companies usually expect to raise capital on debt terms because of the lower risk, but the yield on debt is too low to be of interest to VCs. On the other hand,

leave that one for the NIH

refers to a technology being so early stage that it will require many years of fundamental research and may never work, so it is best left for government funding.

With the basic screening out of the way, it's back to assessing the merits of the proposal. Intuition or a *gut check* tends to be the first real screen for most VCs. It's hard enough to sell any product or service, so if you plan to build a big company with a lot of sales then the

> *value proposition should never be a second order effect.*

This is geek-speak for saying that a product's merit should be obvious. If the product or service being sold has an esoteric utility value where you have to get creative to locate customers that might want it, then you'll likely end up with a company serving a niche market as opposed to a homerun.

As for pondering the overall plan, this goes to the classic question that dates back to 1703:

Will this business hold water?

However, there are some methodical ways to answer this question. You can apply Venture Capital 101 fundamentals such as assessing the management team, market opportunity, and competitive advantage.

Bet on the jockey, not the horse.

*I'd rather have an A-team
with a B-technology than a B-team
with an A-technology.*

A rising tide lifts all boats.

It's like giving sight to the blind.

*God issued them the distribution rights on
air.*

If a plan meets the fundamentals of management, market opportunity, and competitive differentiation then you can start on the less tangible issues such as whether the company can grow and if there is an exit.

Is this a product or a business?

Products address limited markets and often have limited life spans. You'll have a much stronger exit if you have a standalone business that is sustainable. However, sustainability still needs to be augmented with huge growth potential.

Is this a lifestyle company?

A neighborhood gas station is sustainable and can probably keep its owner gainfully employed for many years, but it may never grow into the kind of exit you need to be a successful venture capitalist. The need for growth raises the issue of scalability and other bottlenecks.

Nine women can't make a baby in a month.

Since your primary contribution will be money, the business must be able to leverage capital for growth. A one-of-a-kind goose that lays golden eggs sounds like a great investment but since it will never grow, your capital is useless except to buy the goose at a discount from the owner.

At some point, you'll find it very helpful to meet the entrepreneurs *since a picture is worth a thousand words*. Peter Lynch of Fidelity Investments once commented,

> *"I like to buy a company any fool can manage because eventually one will."*

Even if you have difficulty judging people, you'll at least get a product demo. When meeting in person, you should prepare yourself for the three basic lies that entrepreneurs often tell VCs:

> *1. It's not about money. I want you for your value-add.*
> *2. We won't need more money after this.*
> *3. The product is in beta.*

When translated, it comes out as:

> *1. I'll still respect you in the morning.*
> *2. I got this sales projection from a business plan template.*
> *3. We have a nice brochure and possibly a demo.*

One universal acid test is whether you would invest your own money. As a general partner, you will have to, but as an associate without carried interest, you might encounter opportunities to *cherry pick*. Since the Limited Partners would view cherry picking as a conflict of interest, General Partners are required to co-invest a specified amount (usually 1-2%) on every deal.

Along the way, you'll undoubtedly encounter some *red herrings*.

> *If it's too good to be true, it probably is.*

Green striped deals can also be a distraction. The term refers to an old practice at school admission offices where certain applications were marked for VIP treatment. Since your deal flow network is your lifeblood, be sure to give these deals a careful review and if a turndown is warranted, don't use a form letter. These green stripes can come from within the firm as well.

> *The Managing Partner can turn tar into Teflon.*

Bad deals can gather problems like fur and feathers on tar. As a matter of self-preservation, you should be prepared to acknowledge that you don't always have the answers and that some partners are more equal than others.

Having picked a project to work on, your next step will be to get support within your firm. Getting to know the partners in your firm will come in very handy because their personal comfort zones will vary considerably.

> *Fastball down the middle won't be everyone's pitch.*

Fastballs may have homerun potential but not for everybody. For starters, fastballs aren't that easy to hit, and weaker batters can easily turn them into long fly outs. Similarly, hot deals may not be hot in just anyone's hands since every partner has a unique skill set. Over time, you will observe individual inclinations for deal attributes such as disintermediation, displacing technology, brand equity, para-digm shifts, etc. Nevertheless,

getting the lightbulbs to go off

can be a frustrating process. The difficulty is easily ap-preciated since you'll often have similar reactions when listening to deals found by others in the firm.

The Emperor has no clothes.

I felt like the color-blind man who couldn't see the 7 in the pattern.

On the one hand, these differences in perception are a hassle for entrepreneurs. On the other hand, this is what makes VCs different and thereby allows a wide variety of ideas to get funded. Formula mentality amongst VCs would not only let all the *diamonds in the rough* go unnoticed, but it would also lead to VCs being replaced with mortgage brokers.

DUE DILIGENCE

Having picked a project and gotten sponsorship from your firm, you'll now embark upon the important task of due diligence. The last thing in this industry you want to be known for is

drive-by due diligence.

The quality of your due diligence not only protects your investment but also brands the company for the purposes of raising subsequent rounds of investment. So you should focus on doing a very thorough investigation.

Get your fingerprints onto the murder weapon.

Abraham Lincoln once said that if someone gave him eight hours to chop down an oak tree, he would spend seven hours sharpening his ax.

The easiest way to improve your luck is to stop betting.

There is no reason why high risk has to be associated with gambling if you do your homework. You'll inevitably miss things that you'll come to regret, but knowing not to miss them the second time is intrinsic to the venture capital process.

Experience is what you get when you're looking for something else.

Another mistake would be to view due diligence as only searching for reasons not to do a deal.

> *Don't use facts the way a drunk uses a*
> *lamppost, for support rather than*
> *illumination.*

Since the firm is unlikely to be completely sold on the deal at this point, your due diligence should devote an equal amount of effort to justifying the deal. The process can be frustrating at times.

> *They're standing on the air hose.*

The management and reference checks can all be slow in getting back to you. As your competitors at other firms deal with similar issues, it will be a scramble to find other ways to get the needed information. Your ability to come to a conclusion without becoming a nuisance to the entrepreneurs can be a source of competitive advantage.

Management Team

The single best proxy for a company's likelihood of success is the quality of its management team. It's simply too much work for you to *drag a mediocre team up hill*. An immediate and simple area to examine is how dedicated and qualified is the team. The dot-com boom has generated a lot of opportunity and incentive for under qualified people to bounce from company to company.

> *The team is a mile wide and an inch deep.*

> *Does he have twenty years of experience or*
> *one year of experience twenty times?*

> *Is he a mutual fund employee?*

The latter refers to employees who bounce from one hot company to the next and only stay long enough to vest some stock. One simple screen for the wannabe serial entrepreneur is whether they have *skin in the game.*

> *The chicken was involved but the pig is committed.*

Whether the contribution was an egg or bacon really boils down to whether the entrepreneurs are making a significant personal investment of either cash or intellectual property. Contributing a lot of time is trickier since a lot of people need to be employed somewhere anyway.

The marketplace for any big business opportunity will surely be competitive so your team can use all the relevant experience it can get.

> *A showroom car may look nice but it hasn't been anywhere.*

> *I don't want to pay their tuition.*

It's certainly no fun to be educating the entrepreneurs at your own expense but education is also a strong source of evidence for past achievement. Note that achievement is the key word as opposed to the content of the education which can always be supplemented later in life. Did the individual thrive in a competitive environment? Are they high achievers with a sense of accountability? Due dates, grades, and class leadership are all challenges that schools provide that can be a predictor of future behavior. Needless to say, don't confuse the achievements of the school with the achievements of the individual.

> *You can always tell a Harvard man, but you can't tell him much.*

> *HBS graduates are often wrong but never in doubt.*

> *An MBA's first shock could be the*
> *realization that companies require*
> *experience before they hire a chief*
> *executive officer.*

Nevertheless, the academic pedigree certainly establishes the level of competition a person has faced in the past. In the end, there is no substitute for experience, and the same is true for drive and ambition. You can still supplement an inexperienced team by bringing in *adult supervision*. In general, the skill sets of a CEO will vary by stage.

> *Never bet on a sprinter in a marathon.*

Early stage CEOs usually need to be domain experts and capable of *wearing multiple hats.* The later stage CEO has to be a strong spokesperson for the company and capable of attracting and retaining great managers to scale the company. Assessing leadership is a soft skill that will develop with experience. Fundamentally, leadership is an attribute that is earned and not given.

> *There are only two kinds of people who*
> *fail: those who listen to nobody and those*
> *who listen to everybody.*

> *A leader shouldn't get too far ahead of his*
> *troops or he'll get shot in the ass.*

> *If smoke lays close to the ground, then bad*
> *weather is coming.*

Smoke near the ground literally means a low pressure system, but it also suggests that problems within the rank and file are a sign of trouble for the company.

> *"A full moon blanks out all the stars*
> *around it."*

Ted Turner once said this about himself, but you can use this as a warning sign. Great leaders will surround themselves with greatness and empower those people to succeed. The worst case scenario is having an imposing bozo that has turned his/her troops into yes-men. At the other extreme,

eagles don't flock

so a team of alpha males that all want to lead can also be a problem. There needs to be teamwork and a clear path of accountability so even having the wrong leader is preferable to a power struggle.

You'll also learn a lot by examining the entrepreneur's motivation for becoming one. A Harvard Business School professor once said,

"To understand the entrepreneur, we should look at the juvenile delinquent."

Is this a persistent refusal to conform to conventional thinking or a rebellion against authority? A simple test is to ask:

Would you rather be rich or be king?

Unfortunately, this question is loaded and should be rephrased, "would you rather be your own boss?" Entrepreneurs do enjoy controlling their own destiny but make sure it's financial freedom they seek as opposed to the freedom from accountability.

Success is 1% inspiration and 99% perspiration.

Since it will be a major grind for the entrepreneurs, wealth can always be counted on as a motivator while being your own boss can be an excuse for taking it easy. You'd be surprised how many entrepreneurs want to start their own businesses just to avoid reporting to someone else. It may sound admirable but the attitude doesn't have a good correlation with success if venture capital is involved.

> *That guy was so conceited that he called*
> *Dial-a-Prayer to check for messages.*

Your investment is actually the beginning of a partnership so you need to sense some chemistry and a willingness to accept advice. Good entrepreneurs will acknowledge their limitations and welcome the opportunity for help. This includes bringing in professional management when needed.

Vision and salesmanship are a bit easier to assess and will go a long way towards managing a company as well as attracting future investors.

> *The next time you're in a meeting, look*
> *around and identify the yesbutters, the*
> *notnowers, and the whynotters. Whynotters*
> *move companies.*

That was from a 1984 General Electric advertisement. In general, advertising raises the issue of sales and communication skills. When it comes to categorizing sales people, there are three metaphors: *prospectors, hunters,* and *farmers.* This translates to those who generate leads, those who close new clients, and those who maintain existing accounts. For your startup, pay particular attention to recruiting *coin-operated* hunters.

> *They couldn't even sell water in the*
> *Sahara.*

Or at the other extreme,

> *they could sell hams in a synagogue.*

This last phrase has several implications. A great salesperson is an essential part of a complete management team. However, this phrase also touches upon credibility. Your

CEO should definitely be a great leader who can attract great salespeople but not necessarily be one.

Market Opportunity

Due diligence wasn't meant to be easy, especially when analyzing nascent markets.

> *Nothing worth learning is learned quickly*
> *except parachuting.*

The only thing for certain is that not performing diligence can leave you trying to save your investment. One of the first questions to ask is to establish the type of market play.

> *Is this cheaper-better-faster or*
> *a brave new world?*

If the former, an easy place to start is simply asking customers to compare the new product to whatever they're currently using. Speaking to customers is not only an important part of the diligence process but an opportunity for your own enlightenment. Use this enlightenment to sell the deal to your firm.

> *Is this a must-have or a nice-to-have?*

> *Will the dogs eat the dog food?*

You should be careful with that last one since a successful entrepreneur once mailed an emptied can of smelly dog food to a venture capitalist that turned him down earlier. Even if customers indicate that the new product or service is compelling, you still need to assess their resistance to change. Does the new product require a

> *forklift upgrade*

where a deeply entrenched ERP system has to be thrown out to accommodate the new system? If so, you should make certain the value proposition is strong enough to justify a high price and also be sure to reserve a lot of capital to stay with the company for the many years it might take before becoming successful. Also note whether there is hesitancy about the price or buying from a startup with little or no history.

Can we enter the pool at the shallow end?

Which means they want the lite version of the product with entry-level pricing or perhaps that they only want a test drive. If you get this reaction a lot, be sure that the product and sales model for this company can support rapid, inexpensive deployments.

Experienced entrepreneurs will often have a diligence packet prepared with references from *low hanging fruit* and *love letters* from satisfied customers. However, you should be wary of false positives from early adopters. Geoffrey Moore explains in *Crossing the Chasm* how there will be early adopters of just about anything but there is a chasm that separates them from the mainstream market. This chasm is in part due to the

China Syndrome

which gets misused by entrepreneurs in multiple ways. If a market has over a billion people, you'll find a lot of customers even if the product is desired by only a small fraction of the population. On the assumption that any fool can capture one percent of the market, many business plans start with unrealistically large market sizes and then rely on the China Syndrome for success. However,

execution is everything and anything but trivial.

When it comes to execution, you can put on your business school hat to review the sales and marketing strategy. The old adage of *building a better mousetrap* and expecting the world to beat a path to your door doesn't work.

Mousetraps are sold not bought.

Kevin Costner strategy —Build it and they will come.

That is in fact a *Field of Dreams*. Even with the Internet, customers won't just stumble across a web site very often. Nevertheless, the Internet does offer new strategies that are somewhat passive such as *viral marketing* to promote *killer apps*.

In the case of *brave new worlds* where neither the product nor awareness of it even exists, you need to ask:

Is this evolutionary or revolutionary?

Is this a missionary sale?

In other words, will the customers need to change their behavior? Will the customers know they even have a need for this product? Is this something radically different that will have to be evangelized?

If you're going to be a bridge, be prepared to be walked on.

Expending the effort to educate the public is an inherent risk with being a *pioneer into uncharted territory*. Competitors may ultimately benefit the most from your efforts if you are too early to market.

The cutting edge is good, but the bleeding edge is bad.

Hopefully, a company won't bleed so badly that it dies in the process. Do your best to assess whether the market is ready. After all, we don't want to discourage revolutionary ideas and there can be extraordinary benefits to being first to market.

> *The first man gets the oyster;*
> *the second man gets the shell.*

Ideally, you'll be first to a momentum market where you have a solution to an unsolved problem of broad appeal.

> *In a strong wind, even turkeys can fly.*

> *Find a parade and get in front of it.*

Geoffrey Moore characterizes a momentum market as a *tornado*. It's hard to mess up in a tornado, so not being first isn't necessarily a problem provided you've timed your investment correctly.

Competition

Your management team should go to bed each night worried about how their competitors might *beat 'em like a drum*, and then wake each morning with a renewed sense of purpose.

> *The breakfast of champions is not cereal;*
> *it's the opposition.*

> *Only the paranoid survive.*

The latter was, of course, from Andy Grove. Watch out for management teams that don't believe they have competitors.

> *If the going gets easy, you may be headed*
> *downhill.*

Any market worth pursuing will have competitors. Even if competitors are nascent, a great team will always be concerned and continually raising the barriers to entry. You should perform your own survey of the competitive landscape. This process will not only identify vulnerabilities but it will greatly improve your comprehension of the industry. You'll then know whether there is truly a first mover opportunity to do some

open field running.

One vintage automobile is a collector's item; a 100,000 of them are Edsels.

If there are too many competitors, then find out if it is a fragmented market with no clear leadership or if there are dominant players.

Is there a gorilla in this jungle?

Competing with Amazon.com is like getting into a bleeding competition with a blood bank.

The latter is no longer quite as relevant since Amazon.com became a profitable company, but the statement still pertains to competing with heavily funded competitors. Nevertheless, large competitors may still be vulnerable. Incumbents that have gotten big and slow over the years can be an opportunity for your company to go *white elephant hunting.*

In business, if you insist on following tradition, you'll likely become history.

Some of the best opportunities for entrepreneurs include displacing existing businesses that cannot adapt to change. Amazon.com certainly blazed this trail for future entrepreneurs by establishing the classic example of how electronic commerce can take market share away from traditional *brick and mortar* retailers.

Business Models

Entrepreneurs have always known that a business model can be a competitive advantage. A new business model such as electronic commerce can help a startup

> *catch the competition with their pants*
> *down.*

But it has to be a complete transformation where the incumbent is fundamentally unable to respond.

> *You can't paint zebra stripes on an*
> *elephant.*

Not only is it still an elephant, but everyone will know it's still an elephant. For example, the dot-com transformation for many businesses was over hyped. Having a website instead of a brochure docsn't qualify as a fundamental shift in economics. Similarly, the wave of application service providers (ASPs) providing

> *apps on tap,*

more recently known as *software as a service (SaaS)* for providing a new way to deliver enterprise software, should also be closely scrutinized. In some cases, it is truly a better way to sell and deliver enterprise software. In other cases, it is just a scheme to relocate the server or to charge monthly instead of up front. Another questionable business model that has been over hyped is

> *peer to peer (P2P).*

Always ask yourself whether the company operates better as a P2P company or if they redefined themselves as P2P to improve their appeal to investors. One litmus test might be whether your P2P company has a *path to profitability (P2P)*. On the other hand, a good example of a disruptive shift in business model is what eBay did to newspaper classifieds, which was once characterized as *consumer to consumer (C2C)*.

Embracing the web will be a simple matter of survival for many businesses. From that reality have come several new tactics. Hotmail's use of *viral marketing* made many others consider the strategy. A host of Internet companies have also employed the *West Coast Offense* where the focus is on hype and growth to achieve critical mass while deferring revenue as a secondary concern. The Internet has also made the classic *cocaine business model* very affordable. This involves giving something away to get the customer hooked.

Another classic business model is the Gillette strategy.

Where are the razor blades?

This is where the razor is cheap but all the money is made in selling razor blades. You should use this as a reminder to watch for recurring revenue opportunities.

We'll sell bullets instead of fighting the war.

Let that be a suggestion to not let the big picture distract you from the details. In the early days of the Internet, the battle of the dot-coms had everyone guessing while a lot of recurring revenue was made selling bandwidth. Of course, venture returns call for rapid growth, so the revenue is ideally *big ticket* in price as well as broad in demand. Otherwise the strategy may prolong a slow death.

The pecked to death by ducks strategy.

It's like trying to move a mountain a pebble at a time.

Speaking of broad appeal, the *McDonald's business model* continues to be synonymous with franchising. Broadness can also be addressed by the breadth of a product line.

*Sherwin Williams paint strategy – we'll
cover the world for you*

Technical Due Diligence

With technology remaining the mainstay of venture capital for the foreseeable future, you'll undoubtedly encounter opportunities to perform technical due diligence. The entrepreneurs will claim *cheaper, better, faster* but you'll have to verify to what degree.

*We'll turn blue-chip companies into
buffalo-chip companies.*

Since innovation and entrepreneurship go hand in hand, smart minds will always be searching for displacing technology that can break into lucrative markets. Another issue to address is whether you have a *one trick pony*. Technology can be a basis for a growing business, but a product that cannot scale will not have any successors. A one trick pony can also refer to the risks of only having a single, large customer that is the entire basis for a market.

Is this technology a vitamin or an aspirin?

Both have value but aspirin is worth more because it makes a current problem go away. Vitamins are tougher to sell because it's harder to tell which vitamins work better or if they work at all. Things not working are an unfortunate pitfall of investing in technology. C*rib death* is particularly risky in biotech where both technology and regulatory hurdles need to be overcome. There is no substitute for domain knowledge, but don't shy away from using experts when technology verification is an issue. At times, the technical experts can even be lawyers. Since a technology company's intellectual property will represent a significant portion of its value, you need to thoroughly understand any patent or licensing issues.

Batteries not included.

A right to use a patent may generate the same revenue as owning a patent but there can be a big difference in the ultimate valuation of the company.

Financials

Put on your beanies! You spreadsheet jocks will love this aspect of due diligence because it makes an investment memo look mighty thick and impressive. Furthermore, you can reuse the templates.

Businesses live and die by the numbers.

Orderly financials are not only an indicator of the company's health but also an indicator of whether the management is on top of its business.

Why is there so much month left at the end of our money?

Cash is king for a startup, so run if they have to ask that question. It's a *no-brainer* for later stage companies but it's still an issue for early stage ventures. Even though the forecast usually makes for good fiction, an accurate presentation forces entrepreneurs to understand the revenue objective and expense structure of their business.

A fuzzy target is hard to hit.

Even a small leak can sink a great ship.

Once you have a pro forma, you'll undoubtedly give it the requisite across the board *haircut* as a part of your sensitivity analysis.

A conservative projection is an oxymoron.

Entrepreneurs have a knack for painting downside scenarios as highly desirable outcomes. Web sites on how to prepare business plans probably have *hockey stick* growth curves that can be cut and pasted into business plans.

How big is the handle on the hockey stick?

Starting to look more like a goalie's stick.

The size of the handle addresses the question of total addressable market, which is an important thing to know. Likewise, knowing the location of the *heel* of the stick is the answer to *the $64,000 question,* because it reveals when the company finally gains traction. A similar curve is the *J-curve* which models cash flow and includes a dip below zero in the beginning. *Death Valley* refers to the negative cash flow period on the J-curve that needlessly reminds you that you don't want to stay in Death Valley very long.

Besides determining whether the company is being run properly, you have an overall objective in this exercise of getting a price your firm is willing to pay. Be sure to account for *bluebirds* that make the sales look artificially rosy. An important part of this exercise is knowing the total amount of money that similar companies have required in order to reach an exit event. Then spread that money over several rounds using typical valuation markups such as 2x, 1.5x, and 1.5x for the seed to third rounds.

You can't get there from here.

Earlier isn't always better.

You may find that certain rounds are unachievable because your company won't be worth that much for what it will have accomplished by then. Allow for this by balancing your valuation and transaction size accordingly. Once you're comfortable with the adjusted numbers, you can estimate the return on investment based on valuation comparables and see if the deal passes your firm's *hurdle rate*.

> *This deal is like picking a policeman's pocket.*

It's not enough to just make money; a venture needs a reward that merits the risk. If you find yourself *counting the caribou*, then you're probably on the wrong track.

> *If sophisticated calculations are needed to justify an action, then don't do it.*

The chances of failure are so intrinsically high that you might as well start with things stacked in your favor.

CLOSING THE DEAL

The Decision

So you've been standing around,

> *looking like a kid on a diving board for the first time.*

You can perform due diligence until you're blue in the face, but at some point you'll have to shake the *analysis paralysis* and make a decision.

> *If you take it apart and put it back together enough times, you'll eventually have two of them.*

In other words, you are bound to come up with problems if you over analyze a deal. There are no perfect deals.

> *If deals were perfect, they wouldn't be talking to venture capitalists.*

After all, you are being paid to take risks. If it were a sure thing, entrepreneurs would be talking to bankers or their mothers.

> *So why not go out on a limb? That's where the fruit is.*

> *If Columbus had turned back, no one would have blamed him. No one would have remembered him either.*

These are basically the same as *no guts, no glory,* but they are also reminders that you can't make money without investing it and possibly losing it.

> *You can't make an omelet without breaking*
> *a few eggs.*

Should you choose to take the plunge, rest assured that you're not at the mercy of gravity. One school of thought believes that any deal can be a good deal if the management executes.

> *It's not how the wind blows that matters;*
> *it's how you set the sail.*

The corollary is that even a good deal can be ruined if the management fails to execute.

> *"'cause ev'ry hand's a winner and ev'ry*
> *hand's a loser" – Kenny Rogers*

This applies to your deals as well so

> *don't dwell on the zits and start looking for*
> *ointment.*

Just be wary of the perils of falling in love with your own investment thesis. You may find yourself doing a deal just to justify your own market outlook theory because you've

> *played around in it so much you end up*
> *drinking your own bath water.*

The Turndown

One could argue that this business is more about saying *no* than it is about doing deals. You typically say *no* more than a hundred times for every *yes*. How you handle the turndowns can determine your reputation as much as your deals.

Never fall in love with a deal or a management team. You run the risk of

spinning problems into gold.

Torture the data long enough and it will confess to anything.

There will always be more deals. Just look at your email inbox if you have any doubt. There are many reasons for a deal to *go sour* so rest assured that the few you've already found are plenty enough.

This deal draws flies like week-old sushi.

I can bandage a problem or two, but this company is bleeding from a thousand cuts.

"Know when to walk away, know when to run" – Kenny Rogers

Having decided to pass on a deal, try not to

vote with your feet

by running away like so many of your venture colleagues. Instead, be gracious enough to offer constructive feedback so that the entrepreneur can still walk away grateful.

Any jackass can kick a barn down, but it takes a carpenter to build one.

This is especially true when handling deals that were VIP referrals in need of a *soft landing*. Moreover, you should be cognizant of the fact that reading plans is a lot easier than writing them. Similarly, you should acknowledge your limitations and be humble enough to recognize that you could be wrong.

> *"You miss 100% of the shots you never take" – Wayne Gretzky.*

> *"Big ideas are so hard to recognize, so fragile, so easy to kill. Don't forget that, all of you who don't have them."*
> *– John Elliott Jr., Chairman of Ogilvy & Mather.*

Don't be so jaded about filtering plans that you forget an entrepreneur is showing you his/her personal baby.

> *Keep your words sweet – you may have to eat them.*

> *Did you ever notice that the knockers are always on the outside?*

> *If you enjoy honey, don't kick over the beehive.*

It goes without saying that your deal flow network should be treated well. On the other hand, entrepreneurs will often not listen and persist in trying to convince you. If you *keep the door cracked open* too long, a slow turndown can be worse than *just saying no*.

> *If you want to have short meetings, don't provide chairs.*

> *This deal needs a clean shot to the head.*

If you want to avoid the risk of creating misguided expectations, you need to provide clear feedback. Ambiguous or missing feedback can result in endless follow-up from entrepreneurs despite dismal chances of funding.

Once you've done the dirty deed, don't regret it or dwell on justifying it.

> *We've already said no, let's not have a*
> *funeral.*

There are a lot of eager entrepreneurs still waiting to hear from you and that pile on your desk isn't getting any smaller.

Negotiating

You're still not quite there yet. For that one deal in a hundred that you actually want to do, a lot can still happen before you successfully close it. For starters, you can count on valuation being an issue almost as sure as the sun rises in the morning.

> *If you don't like the size of your slice, then*
> *bake a bigger pie.*

> *It's not the percentage that matters; it's the*
> *price per share.*

Both of which are ways of redirecting attention away from today's reality and towards the desired outcome.

> *You never get quite what you expect so*
> *expect a lot.*

Portfolio theory demands that you expect a lot when investing at high risk. The winners will need to carry the rest of the group. Painting a compelling reason for your position with the entrepreneurs can go a long way towards *cracking the valuation* stalemate since most valuation figures for early stage companies are arbitrary. The size of the likely exit for the type of company in question versus your need to *move the needle* on your megafund can often paint a clear story.

> *Our money is greener than theirs.*

*Most people are willing to meet halfway;
trouble is, most people are lousy judges of
distance.*

*Agreement is brought about by changing
people's minds – other people's.*

On the other hand, good deals come from experienced entrepreneurs who don't come cheap. Moreover, you need to recognize that a loss is a loss at any valuation and a homerun will make any starting valuation look acceptable.

*Something you get for free is usually worth
what you paid for it.*

*If you think you have them eating out of
your hands, it's a good idea to count your
fingers.*

*We're in the business of buying winning
lottery tickets, so what's the difference
whether it costs 50 cents or $1.*

Nevertheless, here are some tidbits on the *art of the deal* if you are struggling with the terms. The general idea is to create leverage by having more information and/or time. Especially since *time is money* and *the clock is ticking* for many entrepreneurs.

Get them to tip their hand.

*When the guy says, "It's now or never,"
always choose, "never."*

*Stonewalling is the last step before caving
in.*

*Cash is like a roll of toilet paper, the closer
it gets to the end, the faster it goes.*

In the course of negotiating with experienced entrepreneurs, you could find yourself becoming a *stalking horse*. In this situation, your offer only serves to set the market price for competing firms who are also stalled in negotiations. The best remedy for this is to have extensive relationships in the venture community so that you can reach out to the existing board members to get the true scoop. We're all in this long term so no one wants to burn the bridges between colleagues.

Finally, never be pressured to finish a deal without adequate due diligence. There will always be more deals. A hot deal on a *short fuse* might not be so hot if a great business relationship isn't worth the wait. Don't lose sight of the fact that you're actually trying to create a partnership.

> *If we build bridges instead of walls, we*
> *could charge tolls.*

Term Sheets

Congratulations, you've agreed on terms so now it's just a matter of finishing the paperwork. Note that the term sheet isn't the actual deal but only the summary document from which the lawyers will generate a mountain of papers called the closing docs. If I ever find the time, a separate tutorial is probably warranted for explaining legal terms such as Participating Preferred for *double dipping* and *full ratchet* for anti-dilution. In any case, the term sheet is just a tool of the trade and not the art itself.

> *A verbal contract isn't worth the paper it's*
> *written on.*

> *Negotiating is a way of saying "nice*
> *doggie" until you can find a rock.*

Term sheets do serve a lot of purposes in addition to establishing contractual terms. Binding term sheets are also a way to lock up a deal until you complete your diligence.

However, you shouldn't get carried away and use a term sheet like a weapon.

Not every wedding can have a pre-nuptial.

You should still keep in mind that a deal is only as successful as the relationship behind it. Before you start signing releases regarding the time your mother dropped you as a child, try to remember that you're a VC and not a lawyer. Lawyers are paid to stay out of court whereas you're paid to deal with ambiguity.

Syndication

If a deal is expensive, you can mitigate your risk through syndication. Doing so allows you to *save dry powder* for later rounds of financing. However, syndicating a seed round where the business model is being refined is not a good idea.

Too many cooks in the kitchen.

The exception to this would be hands-on investors with specific expertise. Especially since private investors often do not *crowd out* the smaller seed rounds. You still need to be aware that

not every angel comes from heaven.

In selecting deal partners, it's best to focus on industry expertise to bring more knowledge and strategic partnerships to the table.

A river is powerful because many drops of water have learned the secret of cooperation.

We can parachute them into this deal.

Expertise also allows a firm to decide more quickly without unnecessarily delaying the closing. When you *tee up a deal* for other firms, it's also considered a networking gesture and an opportunity to have other deals *served up* in return.

Getting a seat at the table.

Play with friends but cut the cards yourself.

When it comes to participating in deals being syndicated by others, keeping your *place at the table* can be a delicate balance but always maintain your ability to perform your own due diligence. The benefit of branding a company's balance sheet with famous venture capital firms as investors also has its drawbacks. The

venture capital shell game

is where problems are hidden from new investors by the glitz of the dealers. During boom times, many companies also became *bandwagons* that benefited from the *snowball effect* of famous investors piling heavily into supposedly hot deals.

Scratching your initials into the side of the Titanic.

In those situations, often no one was in charge but everyone assumed the opposite. This left syndicate members staring at each other with puzzled expressions in search of the reason why they all invested in the first place.

BUILDING A BUSINESS

Don't congratulate yourself too much for getting a deal done; that was the easy part. The long process of building a real company of value starts with joining the team and finding out whether the

vacation matches the brochure.

Recruiting Management

Recruiting is a first on most VC checklists unless you're a late stage investor working on companies that only need capital and come complete with instruction sheets that say *just add water*. One of your first and most common opportunities to add that mythical value is recruiting a CEO and/or the other members of the senior management team. Your firm's reputation and contacts can go a long way towards attracting the best talent. It's especially valuable to be on the short-list with the best executive *headhunters*.

If you're an early stage investor, it's common to have a technical team that lacks experienced business management.

This company needs adult supervision.

Young technical co-founders are often resistant to hiring at any level because they are very picky about needing people as intelligent as themselves and they also want to preserve cash and equity. A simple solution in teaching them to scale is having them *tread water* while

drinking from the fire hose

from all the work that needs to be done at a startup. In other cases, the company may just need a spark. A fresh, outside perspective can often do wonders for a stalled company.

We used to be so inbred it's a wonder we
weren't all three-legged.

However, one caveat for early stage investing is that an outside CEO should not be recruited until after the business model has been validated in order to maximize the likelihood of a good fit. If you do it before the model has been established, then you tend to get the business model of the CEO's former employer. In general, the idea of changing management can be very unsettling to the founders of a company. A forced replacement of management can ruin a company so don't make an investment unless you have buy-in from the entrepreneurs.

Any time you think you have influence; try
ordering around someone else's dog.

If you plan to wound a rhinoceros, you
better have a tree handy.

Regrettably, there will be other occasions when you're hiring a CEO because you first *had to kill one* for underperforming.

The recruiting process itself will involve *kissing a lot of frogs* in search of that *gold plated CEO with the Midas touch.*

The closest to perfection a person ever
comes is when they write their resume.

To a large extent, you can make up for inexperience in judging people by knowing what to ask.

Changing things is central to leadership,
and changing them before anyone else is
creativeness.

When interviewing prospective CEOs, ask for examples of past activities and look for evidence of the ability to change an organization. Another strong indicator of leadership and potential success is a CEO's (or any manager's) ability to recruit past employees, which is known as the *Pied Piper effect*. People rarely quit their jobs to pursue risky startups just to follow a leader unless they have a very strong regard for that person. This kind of active testimonial is much stronger than any reference check can ever be. As for past references, employment at a successful organization doesn't tell the whole story, since a slacker can *ride the slipstream* of an organization with momentum.

> *The easiest way to get a good managerial*
> *job is to have a good managerial job.*

Only with true leadership and creativity can a person both transform and find new success. A side note on your own career planning is the fact that most partners in the VC business were hired as partners. An unfortunate reality is that your easiest path to partnership is to be a good associate at a firm and then be poached by another firm.

Once you've found your candidate, then you get to *stroke the poodle*. The imbalance between talent and money will have you in that occasional sell mode to close a strong CEO.

> *If you pay peanuts, you get monkeys.*

You made a large investment to get into this deal so doing a small one to help you get out only seems logical.

Coaching

The study that formed Onset Ventures showed an 80% correlation between success for a seed stage venture and the full-time availability of a seasoned mentor who was not a part of the management team. Coaching continues after the seed stage as well. There should always be certain board members that fill the CEO's shortcomings and have his/her respect. This can include your own contributions; after all, you do interact with more CEOs in a year than most people will in a career. One of the first traits of a great mentor you'll want to have starts with knowing you have

two ears and one mouth.

Your ability to listen empathetically, as opposed to lecturing, will go a long way towards influencing anyone from a CEO to your spouse. This is especially true when the CEO is a type-A, alpha male who isn't used to being told what to do. Although you want to contribute good ideas, there is the important notion of accountability and ownership. Don't let your mark on a company

become shoe prints up the backs of your management.

At the end of the day, the CEO and the company actually do the work so it's best that they take the credit while you stay content with just influencing.

You can't push people up a ladder

is another way of saying that the CEO needs to recognize his ownership of the challenge. When it comes to giving feedback, it's been said to be

more like an airline captain than an art critic.

A pilot goes through an extensive pre-flight check before each departure. If any problems are found, the request for a remedy is quite specific. On the other hand, checklists can wear out your welcome with a CEO.

You can't keep pulling the flowers to check if the roots are healthy.

So always balance your feedback with praise for what's going right. Ultimately, your CEO is responsible for leadership, problem solving, vision, and the company's image to the outside world. Here is a potpourri of additional management wisdom:

Hiring consultants to solve internal problems is another way of saying that if the employees were any smarter, they wouldn't be working here.

The person who knows how will always have a job. The person who knows why will always be his boss.

Great ideas need landing gear as well as wings.

Never get into an argument with people who buy ink by the barrel. – On dealing with the media

There is only one boss – the customer. And he can fire everybody in the company, from the chairman on down, simply by spending his money somewhere else.

Strategy & Execution

Working with the CEO is good start but you can really make your mark by *rolling up your sleeves and getting your hands dirty*. An opportunity to influence a company's strategy can be your greatest behind-the-scenes contribution.

If you don't know where you're going, any road will get you there.

However, you also need to know where *to draw the line between being a VC and being an entrepreneur.* That said, from strategy to business development, there are plenty of opportunities to contribute. If you remember only one thing, let it be the ability to adapt and adapt quickly.

One second is all it takes for the light to turn green and the car behind you to honk.

You don't drown by falling in the water; you drown by staying there.

Unless you're the lead dog, the view never changes.

Business is like riding a bicycle. Either you keep moving or you fall down.

When skating over thin ice, safety comes from speed.

A rut is a grave with both ends knocked out.

Don't let your companies get into ruts. The original study that formed Onset Ventures also revealed a 90% correlation between success and the company changing its original business model. The ability to adapt to changes in the market will be essential for both survival and industry leadership.

They were rearranging the deck chairs on the Titanic

instead of searching for lifeboats or patching the hole has always been a good metaphor for any company large or small. As anyone in a position of influence should, give your input carefully since smaller companies with limited resources need to focus.

*Startups are more likely to die of
indigestion than starvation.*

*If you chase two rabbits, they'll both get
away.*

Although you intend to add value, some common VC practices are controversial.

*Don't play model trains with your portfolio
companies.*

The practice of linking companies together so that they are forced to do business with each other can be hazardous. Introductions are good, but forced relationships tend to make the entire train move at the speed of the weakest link. You should stick to boondoggles and networking events for your portfolio companies rather than forcing a *keiretsu* mentality.

Another dangerous practice is the relocation of companies for the sake of the investor. If you must move a company, don't let traveling to board meetings be the reason.

You can't grow an oak tree in a flowerpot.

The location of the company can make a big difference. You need access to the right skills and infrastructure. However, it's not a given that everything works better in Silicon Valley.

Here is a medley of additional sagacity:

*Be braver – you can't cross a chasm in two
small jumps.*

*Warranties won't fix manufacturing
problems. The problems need to be fixed in
manufacturing.*

Someday is not a day of the week.
Opportunity is knocking, get to it.

It wasn't raining when Noah built the ark.

Pick battles big enough to matter and
small enough to win.

Board of Directors

The role of the board of directors is to protect shareholder value. Almost all of you work for firms where you prefer to take board seats when making investments. It's an opportunity to *control your own destiny* by influencing the company. The alternative of being a passive investor can save a lot of time but at a price.

They treat me like a mushroom, keep me in
the dark and feed me manure.

The first rule of forming an effective board for a startup is to keep it small. I recommend five or fewer members and, at most, seven as the company matures. Otherwise, you may get *campfire syndrome* where everyone sits around feeling some degree of anonymity. What you really want is a close and productive working relationship.

We didn't all come over in the same ship,
but we're all in the same boat.

Having unified goals is essential so having a *carry on the beach* is not generally in the best interest of the company. That's where an investor keeps their board seat even after selling their interest in the company.

Practically speaking, the board is only responsible for two things: hiring and firing the CEO; and being a sounding board for the CEO. As an effective sounding board, you need to be able to *call a shovel a spade*

quickly. The CEO is the proxy for the company and thereby the vehicle through which the board interacts with the company.

*Is the CEO a thermostat or a
thermometer?*

Don't let the CEO be merely a messenger for the company's report card. What you want instead is a thermostat where the CEO is a mechanism for executing the board's wishes.

*The quality of a board room lunch is
inversely proportional to last quarter's
profitability.*

*The reason dollar bills wear out so quickly
is from all the people passing the buck.*

You'll always hear excuses for missing the plan, but get concerned if your CEO tries to avoid being accountable. Accountability is the only assurance that anything ever gets done. The CEO needs to instill accountability throughout the company and the board needs to instill it in the CEO.

*If you keep pumping air into a flat tire,
you'll still have a flat tire.*

If a company didn't meet plan and needs more money, you need to fix the source of the problem before putting more money into a deal. Anybody can sit on the board of a company that's *on autopilot* but it takes wearing the *black hat* and making tough decisions to justify your presence.

*When elephants fight, it's the grass that
suffers.*

The board's decisions need to be tough and swift. An unresolved struggle can only hurt the company.

EXITING THE INVESTMENT

With a little luck, it will almost be champagne time.

> *Of course luck matters, not having a good
> CEO is bad luck.*

When it comes to liquidating your investment, you're basically looking at going public, an acquisition, a management buyout, or suffering a *fire sale*.

Going Public

Entering the world of investment banking with its *bakeoffs, green shoes, and roadshows* is worth a book in itself. If the IPO market is hot, it will likely be your best outcome.

> *You can only make hay in the sunshine and
> the sun is shining really bright right now.*

> *Carpe diem*

Public markets are beyond your control so *put them on the launch pad* while you can. However, going public isn't a score just yet. You're actually *in the red zone*, so the last thing you want to do is *fumble*. The *touchdown* comes only after surviving the registration period, the stock price swings, and the *lockup* period. If the market is hot, you may even want to hold after the lockup period.

> *Pigs get fat but hogs get slaughtered.*

> *"You got to know when to hold 'em. Know*
> *when to fold 'em." – Kenny Rogers*

Keep a careful watch for the famous *head-and-shoulders* chart pattern which may signify a *bear run* on a speculative stock and leave you waiting hopelessly for a *dead cat bounce*. Timing is everything so use everything you know about the company to do the right thing. Keep in mind that the SEC restricts you to a small *insider-trading window* in which to sell your shares and that your stock may not be liquid due to a limited *float*.

Mergers and Acquisitions

Going public has a lot of drawbacks in the Sarbanes-Oxley era, so acquisitions are often desirable. This is especially true if your company doesn't have a story that's attractive to the public markets but is of strategic interest to a larger corporation. An acquisition also gives you more control over the price and usually offers faster liquidity.

> *Companies aren't sold, they are bought.*

Your company will command a much higher price if it isn't looking for a seller. A second lesson is recognizing that there is a customer in this dynamic, so a compelling value proposition needs to be designed for the purchaser. If you design and manage your investments to be standalone businesses capable of going public, then this won't be an issue. Note that acquisitions are really mergers, which also raises issues. For example, if your company is being bought with the other company's stock, then you may still face price volatility and float risks. Even worse, what if the *marriage* won't work?

> *"Why would Cinderella want to marry a*
> *butcher just because he's got a few yen in*
> *his pocket?"*

This comment came from an analyst discrediting rumors of a merger between Apple Computer and Canon. An acquisition may not be such a clean deal if there is no synergy between the companies. This is especially true if the deal involves stock in the acquiring company or an *earn-out* provision. Both the employees and the markets are efficient about sniffing out a bad deal and will react accordingly.

> *It's like tying two rocks together to see if they'll float.*

The two companies need to add value to each other for the deal to make sense. Having rocks in the first place also raises the issue that acquisitions often have an element of rescue to them. In those situations the

> *light at the end of the tunnel could be a train.*

Remember that many potential acquirers started out as potential competitors. A prolonged due diligence process can lull a company off its guard while waiting for a life saving acquisition that may never consummate. Meanwhile, the due diligence process drains the company of its secrets and distracts management from learning how to survive on their own. At a minimum, never enter a serious M&A discussion without a *breakup fee* in the term sheet. A dreaded situation in which your leverage rapidly evaporates is the

> *musical chairs scenario*

in which several of your competitors have already been acquired and there may only be one remaining chair (prospective acquirer) left in the marketplace. My advice in avoiding this situation is to take Jack Welch's advice of *only building companies that are number one or two in their markets* and not pursuing companies that are *built to flip* (i.e. your investments should be in companies that have the possibility of being standalone entities).

The Fire Sale

> *"Now ev'ry gambler knows that the secret*
> *to survivin' is knowin' what to throw away*
> *and knowing what to keep."*
> *– Kenny Rogers*

Liquidation is never what you originally hoped for but you need to see it as the right thing to do and *not go down with the ship.*

> *If you find yourself in a hole, stop digging.*

Otherwise you're just preparing a grave for what VCs refer to as the *living dead.* The living dead are companies that manage to survive but are not making any progress towards an attractive exit. Instead you should just

> *shoot the dogs and ride the winners.*

> *Trade the horse before it dies.*

> *Stop the cancer before it spreads.*

A deal going south can suck down all of your time as well as your money. It may take some experienced judgment, but knowing when to cut your losses is critical to managing a healthy portfolio. As for supporting those that might still be winners, always adhere to the principles of sunk costs.

> *Don't waste good money trying to save bad*
> *money.*

Treat every follow-on investment as if it were a new one because all investments should stand on their own merits.

RAISING A FUND

Although it's unlikely you'll find yourself raising your own fund any time soon, it's very likely that you'll help your firm raise a new fund. Doing so means coming full circle and experiencing the *tin cupping* that entrepreneurs go through everyday. You'll discover that limited partners (LPs) often

have deep pockets but very short arms,

just like their VC counterparts. Like many hip-shooting VCs in board rooms or poorly prepared entrepreneurs at a pitch, you'll also experience the consequences of

listening with your mouth.

There will be many striking similarities between your fund's offering memorandum and your typical private placement memorandum from a startup. The same goes for the grueling *roadshow.* Fortunately, by this time you'll be armed with best practices from having seen so much capital being raised.

When they pass the hors d'oeuvres, take one because the tray may not come around again.

Raise money while the market is hot so you can ride out the dry spells. The exception is if you manage an *evergreen fund,* where you recycle the profits and avoid fundraising. Even if you don't work for an evergreen fund, a typical fund agreement will still include a *recycling* provision where you can reinvest liquidity proceeds in hopes of driving a higher return. LPs are usually fine with the idea of *letting it ride* because more capital is put to work without increasing the management fees. This may sound pretty good but *one thing you can't recycle is wasted time.*

This emphasizes the fact that the *clock is ticking* already with respect to the IRR calculation on your fund performance. Bottom line is that you definitely don't want to be stuck between funds in a dry market. Before you get paranoid about a dry market killing the VC business, note that venture capital has been described as

the pilot light of American industry.

As such, there will always be some support for this asset class. Although in hard times this support can often be a flight to safety.

No one ever got fired for buying IBM.

The fleeing from unproven managers may happen even if it means giving out *mulligans* to famous funds for a *bad vintage year* when the whole industry lost money. Until you have a brand with a lot of *Roman numerals* behind it, your success in this process is all about track record.

Open up the kimono.

Fund managers and *gatekeepers* will say *show me the money* by asking you to open up your books. They'll compare your records with the actual distributions experienced by your current LPs, so don't get caught *cherry picking* deals the way a first-time fund might. This will also be your motivation for effectively managing your quarterly board reports.

*"You never count your money while you're
sittin' at the table." – Kenny Rogers*

Counting may or may not actually jinx the outcome of your deals but it certainly can't help. Take this as a lesson to not write up the board reports to reflect unsubstantiated gains, because you may find yourself in an embarrassing *write down* that could strain your credibility. Right behind your track record in importance to LPs are the people in the fund. One important aspect of your people story is having a team that's been together for awhile. LPs have been particularly concerned about the rash of partnership meltdowns that have resulted from disputes over economics, strategy, and/or leadership transition.

> *A partnership is like a marriage without*
> *the sex.*

Although there isn't much else you can do to change your resumé or personality, there is always an opportunity to refine your fund strategy. The next most important item for LPs is having a differentiated strategy and a proven history of executing it. In any case,

> *Say it, Live it, Do it*

summarizes the situation as strategy, people, and track record.

The fundraising process is an attorney rich activity. You'll find yourself in a myriad of *clawbacks*, LLCs, LLPs, and *blue sky* laws that are yet another opportunity for a book. One important item to consider is the *joint and several* clause in your fund agreement. When dealing with clawbacks and other liabilities, your LPs will want your firm to have the

> *Three Musketeers Syndrome – One for All*
> *and All for One*

which means that each partner is financially responsible for the collective group in case one or more partners becomes unaccountable for some reason. If your track record isn't enough leverage to avoid the Three Musketeers Syndrome, you can try to offer more *skin in the game* by increasing the percentage contribution that the partners make in the fund itself. In any case, I'd recommend using a law firm that specializes in establishing venture capital partnerships as opposed to your normal investor counsel used on closing investments.

One day you may want to break away and raise your own fund. At least you'll have had a lifetime of getting comfortable with the idea that

size doesn't matter.

You can spin this smaller fund size to your advantage by focusing on fewer deals, more value-added opportunities, and the greater chance of a high return on capital. When you successfully complete this process for yourself, you'll then finally *eat what you kill*. Congratulations will be in order as you'll be known as a *been there, done that* venture capitalist!

DEFINITIONS

1. **ad·age** (²dˋ¹j) *n.* **1.** A saying that sets forth a general truth and that has gained credit through long use.
2. **ap·o·thegm** also **ap·o·phthegm** (²pˋ…-thμm″) *n.* **1.** A terse, witty, instructive saying; a maxim.
3. **aph·o·rism** ('a-f&-"ri-z&m)*n.* **1.** a concise statement of a principle. **2.** a terse formulation of a truth or sentiment : adage
4. **ax·i·om** ('ak-sE-&m) n. **1.** A maxim widely accepted on its intrinsic merit.
5. **max·im** (m²kˋs¹m) *n.* **1.** A succinct formulation of a fundamental principle, general truth, or rule of conduct.
6. **met·a·phor** (mμtˋ…-fôr″, -f …r) *n.* **1.** *Abbr.* **met. metaph.** A figure of speech in which a word or phrase that ordinarily designates one thing is used to designate another, thus making an implicit comparison, as in *" a sea of troubles "* or *" All the world's a stage "*
7. **mor·al** (môrˋ…l, m ¼rˋ-) *n.* **1.** The lesson or principle contained in or taught by a fable, a story, or an event. **2.** A concisely expressed precept or general truth; a maxim.
8. **prov·erb** ('prä-"v&rb)*n.* **1.** a brief popular epigram or maxim : adage

From the *Merriam-Webster* and *American Heritage*
dictionaries.

BIBLIOGRAPHY

Blackburn, D. 1998. *Capturing Life's Opportunities.* Kauffman Fellows II Field Project: Kauffman Fellows Program.

Boone, L. 1992. *Quotable Business: over 2,500 Funny, Irreverent, and Insightful Quotations About Corporate Life.* New York: Random House.

Dickson, P. 1996. *The Official Rules at Work: the Principles, Maxims, and Instructions that Define Your Life on the Job.* New York: Walker Publishing Company.

Gladstone, D. 1988. *Venture Capital Investing: The Complete Handbook for Investing in Small Private Businesses for Outstanding Profits.* Englewood Cliffs, NJ: Prentice Hall.

Gladwell, M. 2005. *Blink: The Power of Thinking Without Thinking.* Little, Brown and Company, Time Warner Book Group.

Kipfer, B. 1994. *Bartlett's Book of Business Quotations.* Canada: Little, Brown & Company.

Larsen, M. 1995. *Oddball Sayings, Witty Expressions & Down Home Folklore: A Collection of Clever Phrases.* San Jose, CA: R&E Publishers.

MCR Software. 1997. *Small Business Wisdom.* Oakland, CA: http://www.quotations.com

Moore, G. 1995. *Crossing the Chasm: Marketing and Selling High-Tech Products to Mainstream Customers.* New York: Harperbusiness.

Moore, G. 1995. *Inside the Tornado: Marketing Strategies from Silicon Valley's Cutting Edge.* New York: Harperbusiness.

Moran, R. 1998. *Fear No Yellow Stickies.* New York: Fireside.

Parietti, J. 1997. *The Book of Truly Stupid Business Quotes.* New York: HarperCollins.

Pentz, C. 1990. *The Complete Book of Zingers.* Wheaton, IL: Tyndale House Publishers.

Phillips, M. 1993. *Good Things to Remember: 333 Wise Maxims You Don't Want to Forget.* Minneapolis, MN: Bethany House Publishers.

Rees, N. 1991. *The Phrase that Launched 1,000 Ships.* New York: Dell Publishing.

Rogers, K. 1978. *The Gambler.* Dreamcatcher Records.

Rybolt, R. 1994. *No Chairs Make for Short Meetings and Other Business Maxims from Dad.* New York: Penguin Books.

Smart, G. 1998. *The Art and Science of Human Capital Valuation.* Chicago: ghSMART.

Tempest, N. and Roberts, M. 1998. *ONSET Ventures, HBS Case No. N9-898-154.* Boston: Harvard Business School Publishing.

Timmons, J. 1996. *New Venture Creation: Entrepreneurship for the 21st Century.* New York: McGraw-Hill.

Wastholm Media. 1997. *Aphorisms Galore.* http://www.aphorismsgalore.com

INDEX

T

U

V

Index